your Truth only. dn Jesus name dpray.

Transforming Your Territory Through Prayer- Walking

Taking Your City Step By Step

David R. Hibbert

Destiny Media Productions
Brossard, Quebec, Canada

Transforming Your Territory Through Prayer-Walking
Taking Your City Step By Step
© 2017 by David R. Hibbert

Destiny Media Productions
P.O. Box 30504
Brossard, Quebec, Canada J4Z 3R6
(450) 676-6944
Email: resource@destinyresource.ca
Website: www.destinyresource.ca

ISBN Paperback Book: 978-1-988738-24-6
ISBN Digital Book: 978-1-988738-25-3

Cover design by Melissa Baker-Nguyen of Lost Bumblebee Graphics. Address inquiries to lostbumblebee@gmail.com.

Requests for translating into other languages should be addressed to Destiny Media Productions.

AMP – Bible quotations marked AMP are taken from the Amplified® Bible, Copyright © 2015 by The Lockman Foundation, La Habra, CA 90631. All rights reserved. (www.Lockman.org). Used by permission.

ERV – Bible quotations marked ERV are taken from the Holy Bible: Easy-to-Read Version, copyright © 1987 by World Bible Translation.

Table Of Contents

Introduction

In this short book, I want to teach you about one of the most powerful tools that God had given to us, that we can use to bring about supernatural transformation.

This tool is a God-given strategic resource that you can use to:

* Change the spiritual atmosphere in your home, neighbourhood and workplace.

* Exercise your spiritual authority over the realm that God has called you to.

* Pull down spiritual strongholds and barriers wherever you go.

* Set your loved ones spiritually, physically, and emotionally free.

The problem is that because we do not understand this powerful tool, we do not use it correctly, or effectively, and as a result, we usually see very limited results.

This tool from God is called "Prayer-Walking".

Unfortunately, when we ask most people what prayer-walking is, they usually reply …. "uhhh …. Praying while walking?"
Yes, it is that, but it is actually so much more!

And as we begin to understand what Prayer-walking really is, we'll start to use it wherever we go … on our street, in our car, on our bus, at our workplace, in our schools, in our malls, in our parks … in fact, the opportunities to use this powerful tool are almost limitless!

So, let us begin by looking at four Biblical foundations for Prayer-Walking.

Part 1 – Why Prayer-Walk?

The Biblical Foundations Of Prayer Walking

1. The Foundation Of Inspired Revelation

Genesis 3:8, NIV – *(8) Then the man and his wife heard the sound of the LORD God as he was <u>walking in the garden</u> in the cool of the day …*

The day after Adam and Eve sinned and ate from the tree of the knowledge of good and evil, and were hiding from God, God came walking in the garden, looking for Adam and Eve.

Why was God walking and looking for Adam and Eve? Because they had a daily routine. Every day, it would seem, God and Adam and Eve would walk together in the Garden of Eden, and talk, and fellowship together.

And they discussed things together, and shared together, and communicated together, and they received revelation from God.

And that is one of the things that prayer walking is – talking WITH God while walking … sharing our hearts with God, speaking to Him, and listening to Him, and learning what He wants us to understand.

What does He want to tell us about our neighbourhood, our workplace, our school? And what does He want us to pray for?

One of the foundations of prayer-walking, is the foundation of inspired revelation. As we walk, we just talk to God, and listen to God, and hear what He wants to tell us about the place where we are walking.

2. The Foundation Of Territorial Possession

Deuteronomy 11:22-24, NIV – (22) If you carefully observe all these commands I am giving you to follow — to <u>love the LORD your God</u>, to <u>walk in all his ways</u> and to <u>hold fast to him</u> — (23) then the LORD will drive out all these nations before you, and you will dispossess nations larger and stronger than you. (24) <u>Every place where you set your foot will be yours</u>: Your territory will extend from the desert to Lebanon, and from the Euphrates River to the western sea.

The land that God was giving them would extend from the Euphrates River (in the east), to the "western sea" (the Mediterranean Sea). What an amazingly big piece of land!

And do you see what God is telling the Israelites (and us)? We will be able to drive out our spiritual enemies before us, and displace or dispossess them, even if they are larger and stronger than us! But there are four very important conditions that we must fulfill, in order to receive this promise of occupying our territory.

First – intensely love God. They had to love the Lord their God.

Second – Live in obedience to God. They had to walk in all of His ways.

Third – Trust God completely. They had to "hold fast" to Him; to follow Him and trust Him no matter how difficult it was.

Fourth – Walk out their territory. They had to claim every place where they were setting their feet. They were to walk out the full piece of territory that God was giving to them.

In Genesis 18, the boundaries of the land that God was giving them were made even clearer.

Genesis 15:18, NIV – *(18) On that day the LORD made a covenant with Abram and said, "To your descendants I give this land, from the river of Egypt to the great river, the Euphrates – (19) the land of the Kenites, Kenizzites, Kadmonites, (20) Hittites, Perizzites, Rephaites, (21) Amorites, Canaanites, Girgashites and Jebusites."*

So according to the Bible, God wanted to give the Israelites a massive amount of land. This land would extend from the river of Egypt (the Nile River) in the South-west, to the Euphrates River in the North-east. (Refer to the picture below.) That land was to include all of present-day Jordan, over half of Syria, just under half of Iraq, and the eastern part of Egypt.

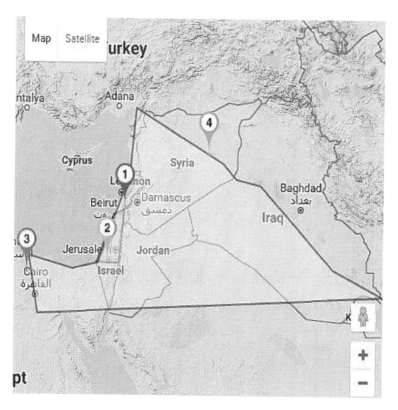

But remember ... they had to walk out the land!

Sadly, according to history, the Israelites only walked out the land to the boundary of Dan in the north (# 1 on map) and Be'er Sheva in the South (# 2 on map).[1]

So, guess how much land they actually possessed? The land that they walked out.

God told the Israelites to walk the land that He wanted to give to them, and as they did so, they were to claim the land for God ... but tragically, they never did!

What does that have to do with us today? God wants us to prayer-walk our streets and claim them in the name of the Kingdom of God. God wants us to prayer-walk our schools and claim them in the name of the Kingdom of God. He wants us to prayer-walk our movie theatres, and our government offices, and so many more places, and claim them in the name of the Kingdom of God.

Whenever God tells us that something is ours, we must walk it out, and claim it for the Kingdom of God.

"Every place where you set your foot will be yours."

Are we walking out the territory that God has told us is ours, or have we decided it is too much work, and so we are willing to settle for so much less than our full inheritance?

3. **The Foundation Of Identificational Repentance**

A foundation that very few talk about, or seem to understand, is the foundation of indentificational repentance.

Genesis 2:7, NIV – *(7) The LORD God formed the man from the <u>dust of the ground</u> and breathed into his nostrils the breath of life, and the man became a living being.*

That phrase "Dust of the ground" literally means "dirt out of soil". In our physical essence, we are made from dirt.

Adam was formed from the dirt, and ever since then, whether we like it or not, because we are made from the dirt, our spiritual life influences the condition of us, and the dirt around us.

Genesis 3:17, NIV – *(17) To Adam he [God] said, "Because you ... ate from the tree about which I commanded you, 'You must not eat of it,' "<u>Cursed is the ground because of you</u> ...".*

God said that because Adam, who was made from the ground, sinned against God, and so received a curse, the ground from which Adam was made, shared in the curse. The Bible does not say that God cursed the earth – it says the earth experienced a curse because of Adam and his sin.

When Cain killed his brother Abel, that sin affected the ground. That is why the Bible says,

Genesis 4:10, NIV – *(10) The LORD said, "What have you done? Listen! Your brother's blood cries out to me <u>from the ground</u>. (11) Now you are under a curse and <u>driven from the ground</u> ...*

The ground did not want Cain to stay there, because the murderous spirit in his heart was affecting the earth. So, Cain was "driven from the ground". He was not driven from all of the ground, since as a human, he still had to walk on the earth. But he was driven from the ground on which he had killed Abel.

That is why the Bible says,

Romans 8:19-21, NIV – *(19) The creation waits in eager expectation for the sons of God to be revealed. ... (21) that the creation itself will be liberated from its bondage to decay ...*

Creation – the earth – is in bondage to decay because of the sin of Adam, and is waiting for us, Adam's descendants, to repent of our sins and mature in Christ. Because as we are revealed as God's mature children, conforming to the image of Christ, the earth itself will be healed and set free from its curse.

That is why, around the world, whenever there is a movement of national repentance of sin (such as documented in the "Transformation" videos), it is accompanied by supernatural harvests of fruits, vegetables, crops, and even fish harvests. As we are healed, the ground around us is healed.

If we do not repent on behalf of the sins that people have committed in our region, it will result in a continued curse on the land in our city, province, or country.

So, whenever we prayer-walk, we need to first cleanse our own hearts and deal with any unconfessed sin, so that we do not bring more damage to the spiritual condition of the land. (There is nothing like spiritually polluting the very ground that we are trying to cleanse).

Then we should ask forgiveness on behalf of any known sins done in the place we are walking, as well as be open to God giving us new revelation on things that we need to repent on behalf of. This is a major component of prayer-walking if we indeed want to see our territory transformed.

4. The Foundation Of Spiritual Warfare

Joshua 6:2-5, NIV – *(2) Then the LORD said to Joshua, "See, I have delivered Jericho into your hands, along with its king and its fighting men. (3) <u>March</u> around the city once with all the armed men. Do this for six days. (4) ... On the seventh day, <u>march</u> around the city seven times, with the priests blowing the <u>trumpets</u>. (5) When you hear them sound a <u>long blast</u> on the trumpets, have all the people give a <u>loud shout</u>; then the wall of the city will collapse and the people will go up, every man straight in."*

What a strange set of instructions! God said that He had already given the Israelites the city of Jericho, but to possess it they had to march around the city once each day for six days, and on the seventh day, march around the city seven times, then blow their trumpets, then give a loud shout, and the city would collapse.

What was going on? They were doing spiritual warfare, while prayer-walking.

As they were walking around the city, once each day for six days, they were thanking God for the fact that God had already given them the land. Then, on the seventh day, they were to blow the trumpets.

Whenever trumpets were blown, it either symbolized a call to assemble together in unity, or to march into war. In this case, I think it was both. They were to be united in their commitment to take Jericho, and they were to understand that this marching was actually warfare, that God was calling them to.

Then they were to give a long blast on the trumpets, symbolizing the moment of victory, and then they were all together to give a loud shout. A loud shout in the Bible always symbolized a joyful celebration of victory.

So, God was telling them, that as they marched around Jericho, they were to declare that Jericho belonged to them. Then they were to use their trumpets to symbolize a united call to warfare, ending with a shout of victorious celebration.

The call to united warfare was immediately followed by a shout of victorious celebration. Why? Because it was the Lord who was fighting the battle, they were just declaring what He was doing, and celebrating His victory.

So, another foundation of prayer-walking, is spiritual warfare. When we prayer-walk, we are to thank God that He is giving us the land that we are walking. We are to understand that we are doing spiritual warfare as we walk. And we are to declare that God is breaking down strongholds, and barriers, and giving us victory.

How Should We Prayer-Walk?

So, using these four Biblical foundations for prayer-walking, let us develop a prayer-walking strategy.

1. Identificational Repentance

First each member of the prayer-walking team needs to pray a cleansing prayer of personal repentance for any unconfessed sin before we walk, so that we do not add any defilement to the land.

Then we should pray prayers of repentance on behalf of the sins that we know are taking place in our territory. It could be due to unrighteous politicians, corrupt law enforcement, drug, and sex trafficking … anything we know that is not righteous.

And we should be open to additional things that God wants us to ask forgiveness for, on behalf of the area where we are prayer-walking.

2. Inspired Revelation

As we walk, we need to keep asking God, "God, what do you want me to pray over this neighbourhood, this house, this business, this school, this church, this playground?" And then we pray for THOSE things. Not my will, but His will. Not my agenda, but His agenda.

3. Spiritual Warfare

As part of spiritual warfare, we must make sure that we are in right relationship with the person we are prayer-walking with, so that we can prayer-walk from a place of unity. In the place of unity, God commands a blessing (Psalm 133:1, 3).

Then we should declare that strongholds must come down, in Jesus' name. Resistance must be broken, in Jesus' name. Spiritual blindness must go, in Jesus' name. Spiritual sight must come.

At the same time, we should be thanking God for the victory that He is working in the place we are prayer-walking.

4. Territorial Possession

We should claim every place where we are walking, for the Kingdom of God. If He is leading us to prayer-walk that territory, it is because He wants us to take it back for Him. We need to declare that that school, that playground, that place belongs to God.

Then, using our spiritual authority, we need to displace, or dispossess our enemies. We command the drug traffickers, and sex traffickers, and pedophiles, and rapists, and stalkers, and gang members to leave in Jesus' name. We command prejudism, racism, and all strife must leave in Jesus' name. Because those places where we are walking are now dedicated to the rule of the Kingdom of God.

How Should We Not Prayer-Walk?

Some things we should NOT do.

1. Do not pray the problem ... pray the solution

God already knows the problem, so do not bother wasting your breath telling God how bad the neighbourhood is. Also, by praying the problem, we magnify and entrench the problem.

Instead, pray the solution. "Thank You God, that You are touching hearts, You are healing lives, You are changing the atmosphere. ..."

2. Do not condemn ... speak blessing

Do not condemn the people in the place you are prayer-walking.

Romans 12:14, NIV – *"... bless and do not curse."*

Instead, speak blessing. Bless the discouraged, bless the children, bless the families, bless homes with the peace of God. Bless civic leaders with righteous wisdom.

3. Do not get sidetracked ... stay focused

When you are prayer-walking, do not get side-tracked by what you have to do after you are finished. Do not allow your mind to daydream. Do not start building a snowman, if you are prayer-walking in the winter. Do not start shopping for shoes or a coat if you are prayer-walking in a shopping mall.

Instead, stay focused on what you are doing ... interceding for your street, your neighbourhood, your workplace, your school.

Other Tips

1. Pray With A Partner

Praying with a partner keeps you focused on prayer.

2. Pray Out Loud If Possible

Praying out-loud helps you to pray with more clarity.

3. Pray With God's Spirit

Let the Holy Spirit lead you as you pray. Pray what He directs you to pray, even if you do not understand it.

4. Pray With God's Word

Declare Scriptures over the area you are prayer-walking, especially scriptures relevant to that area, and scriptures that declare victory. If nothing else, pray "Your Kingdom come, Your will be done on earth as it is in heaven".

5. Take Notes

Take a small pad of paper and a pen with you, and record any insights you receive, so that you can debrief if you are part of a larger prayer-walking team, and to help you continue to pray for that area once you are back home.

Please note that in the winter, the ink in certain pens may become thick, and stop working. So, a felt-tipped pen might work better in the winter.

6. Be Persistent

Do not just prayer-walk a place once, go to the same place a number of times. We have all heard stories of "instant success". However, they really are few in number.

Remember that the Israelites had to prayer-walk thirteen times around Jericho before the walls fell. In the same way, it usually takes ten to twenty prayer-walks in the same place, before you start to see lasting results.

In a home, you may need to prayer-walk the same home every day for two to four weeks, before you see a dramatic change.

On your street, you may need to prayer-walk night after night for a month or more, to see the transformation you are looking for.

Instead of prayer-walking a couple kilometres or miles of streets, it is much more effective to select one short city block, and prayer-walk around it over and over, until you see change.

P u s h   pray until something happens

Summary

So, what is prayer-walking? Prayer-Walking is "Praying on-site, with insight". Prayer-walking is "Praying in the very places that we expect God to manifest His answers".

However, for prayer-walking to be effective, prayer-walking must include these four foundations.

1. Identificational Repentance.

We must repent of our own unconfessed sin, and then repent of behalf of the evil being done in the place where we are walking.

2. Inspired Revelation

We must seek God's insight for the place where we are walking.

3. Spiritual Warfare

We must pull down strongholds in the place where we are walking.

4. Territorial Possession

We must claim the territory for the Kingdom of God in the place where we are walking.

Part 2 – A Corporate Example Of Prayer-Walking

Details Of One Prayer Walk

Our local church does regular prayer-walks in our community, as well as encouraging our members to prayer-walk their homes, neighbourhoods, places of business, schools, parks, and shopping malls.

In Part 3 we will share with you, testimonies of how prayer-walking has made a difference.

First, however, let us share with you a practical example of a resent corporate prayer-walk.

Just eight days ago, as of the time of this writing, we had four teams go out and prayer-walk in the area immediately around our church building.

Instead of praying over a large section of our community (which is what we used to do, with minimal results), this time we had each team of two walk around the same small section as many times as possible, in the time allotted. Each small section of connected streets took approximately fifteen minutes to prayer-walk around, which meant we could walk around them four times in an hour, or six times in ninety minutes.

Briefing

First, we arrived at our designated meeting place, stood in a circle, and reminded the teams of our four-step strategy.

Then we handed out the small notebooks, and pens, and prayer-walking maps which highlighted the area that each team was to prayer-walk around.

This briefing only took approximately seven minutes.

Identificational Repentance

Then we took time for the team to silently repent for all unconfessed sin, so that we did not pollute the ground that we would be walking on with our unconfessed sin.

Then we took time to verbally repent on behalf of all known sin being done in the area.

Then we asked God for additional things that He wanted us to repent from, and we prayed about them.

In total, the identificational repentance only took approximately eight minutes.

Inspired Revelation

Then, for the next sixty minutes (a shorter walk since it was winter) we sent out four teams of two people to prayer-walk four areas that we felt that God wanted us to prayer-walk around.

The teams were encouraged to ask God exactly what He wanted them to pray for. During the course of that hour, teams received general insights to pray for, as well as specific insights for specific homes, impressions of what God was doing, insights into additional strongholds that we had not considered, and other words and images of issues to pray for.

Spiritual Warfare

As the teams prayer-walked, they commanded spiritual eyes to be opened, spiritual blindness to be healed, and spiritual walls and barriers to come down. As well, they were led to pray for such things as peace over the homes, open hearts in the people, spiritual hunger for the people, and for Jesus to reveal Himself to them in dreams.

As one team was praying for hearts to be open, a car stopped beside them, and a person asked for directions to a specific street. Since the team had their prayer-walk map, they showed the driver the street, and then gave them the map. The driver asked what the team was doing. The team told them that they were walking around the street, asking God to bless the people in the homes. The driver then asked where our church was meeting on Sunday, and the team gave the driver directions. Before the driver left, the team was also invited to pray for health for the driver and speak a blessing over them. When you pray for open hearts, God opens hearts!

Territorial Possession

As the teams prayer-walked, they claimed the streets and parks for God. They then commanded demonic spirits and workers of evil to leave the area, since the area belonged to God. One team felt led to spiritually rename a park known as "Villiers Park" to "Shalom Park", and we are waiting to see what happens in the future as a result.

The tallest landmark in our area is the top of a Buddhist temple, and so one team felt led to pray that the cross on the church building next to it would become the new focal point of the neighbourhood, and that people would be blinded to the landmark of the Buddhist temple.

Debrief

After one hour of prayer-walking around their assigned areas as many times as possible, the teams returned to our gathering place for a debriefing (and for some warm hot chocolate since it was winter).

We shared our insights, and our testimonies. Then we closed in prayer, spiritually "sealing" the work that God had done in our area that night, through our obedience to prayer-walking, and thanking God for the fruit that we expect to see in the coming weeks.

Part 3 – The Power Of Prayer-Walking

In this chapter, I want to share with you some personal stories of how prayer-walking has made a difference, so that you can develop your own strategies for prayer-walking in specific places, or for specific situations.

1. Workplace

Before I became involved in full-time Christian ministry, I worked as an electrical-mechanical maintenance engineer for a major industry in Hamilton, Ontario, Canada.

I had promised God, that if He would give me favour in the company, that no matter what department I was transferred to, I would do my best to make sure that everyone in that department had heard the gospel.

I was transferred into one department, and right away I discovered an incredible resistance to the gospel, and a sense of heaviness and discouragement in the whole department. There was also a great lack of cooperation between the disciplines in the department (the electrical and mechanical and civil engineers did not cooperate much with each other).

So, I started to ask around, and I discovered there had been a major layoff about a month before I had been transferred into the department, and many people were feeling discouraged for losing close friends. That was the source of a lot of the heaviness and discouragement.

I also discovered that a couple of years previously, there had been a group of Christians in the department, who had asked for permission to have a Bible study during their one-hour lunch break. However, over the months that sixty-minute Bible study became seventy minutes, then eighty minutes, then ninety minutes and more. When they were rightly asked to shorten their Bible study back to the agreed upon sixty minutes, instead of complying, they cried "religious persecution". So, the floor manager was forced (rightly, in my opinion) to shut it down completely.

Unfortunately, as a result, Christians were given a really bad reputation and were being held in contempt as lazy and uncommitted to the company (as well as thieves, for stealing company time).

I asked God for a strategy on how to change the atmosphere and did what I felt He was leading me to do.

So, I started going into the office twenty minutes early every morning.

First, I repented on behalf of the Christians who misused their privileges.

Then, as I walked around the floor, I would command the heaviness to lift off of the department. I would ask God to help the Christians become good witnesses for Christ. I would dedicate that department to the Kingdom of God. And I would ask God to give me specific things to pray for, as I walked by each desk -- specific things to pray for each worker, supervisor, and manager. And along the way, God even gave me additional strategies about how to gain more favour at work.

Nothing changed for the first couple of weeks, but I refused to give up. By the third week, the atmosphere seemed less heavy, and a couple of Christians came out of hiding, and introduced themselves to me, and we started praying together, and cooperating with each other.

After about six weeks, the heaviness was completely gone, and as the other engineers saw us Christians cooperating together, they started to cooperate also.

After about two months, the contempt against Christians was broken, and we had so many opportunities to share our faith with our co-workers, supervisors, and even our managers that we were absolutely amazed!

And, as a by-product of the new spirit of cooperation in our department, productivity went up, and we were given a special recognition from management because of the change in our department.

2. Home

A number of years ago, a man in our congregation came to me, and shared that two of his young-adult children living at home were involved in drug abuse, alcoholism, and sexual immorality. He had commanded them, pleaded with them, and threatened them to stop, but nothing had worked. And his home was full of strife on a daily basis.

So, first, I implored him to stop threatening and verbally abusing his children. Then, I encouraged him to repent for the way he had treated them, and for not being the supportive and loving father that they needed him to be.

Then, I challenged him to prayer-walk around his house each morning after his children left for work, and to pray God's peace in every room, especially the bedrooms of his children.

I also told him to command all demonic spirits to leave, that had been brought home by his children, and to claim his children for God's Kingdom, and to pray whatever else God showed him.

Then, after the children went to bed each night, he was to quietly lay his hand on their bedroom doors, and pray God's peace for each child, and to again claim them for God's Kingdom.

After about two weeks of doing this EVERY day, the strife in the home started to go down, and they started to treat each other with some respect. Within about four weeks, there was a tangible peace in the whole house, and almost all arguments had ceased.

And by the end of two months, the two children had both recommitted their lives to Christ, broken off some bad relationships, and were free of drug and alcohol abuse.

3. Neighbourhood

A number of years ago, I challenged my home group to start prayer-walking their street every night, just before or just after supper. That meant just one street, of about thirty to forty houses.

Again, we repented for not being a light in our neighbourhood, and then we repented on behalf of all known evil being done on our street. Then we asked God to reveal any evil being done in the homes, and we prayed against it, and we started to speak a blessing over each home, and we claimed our street for the Kingdom of God.

Within just one week, we heard testimonies of neighbours becoming open to hear the gospel. After about two weeks, the late-night weekend noise started to go down, and the noise of family conflict in homes went quiet. On one street, a man was arrested for selling drugs.

After about three weeks, a few of our members were able to bring their neighbours to a church service with them, and a month or so after that, one of the marijuana grow-ops on our street was exposed, raided by police, and shut down.

4. Community Park

My son-in-law organized a one-day, skateboard completion in a park in his area in British Columbia. This park was known for having a lot of crime, and especially drug trafficking.

While the completion was going on, he assigned a number of people to prayer-walk through the park, for the whole day, blessing the children, praying for safety, and praying against the crime that was taking place in the park.

Not only was the event a wonderful success, but within just a few days, a couple of the top drug pushers were arrested in the park, and their operations were shut down.

The police officer for that area, who had originally been resistant to what my son-in-law was doing, contacted him and told him that he would be one hundred percent behind whatever he wanted to do in that area in the future.

5. Mental Illness

For a couple of years, I worked as the director of a forty bed men's mission in a mid-sized community in Ontario, Canada. When I was hired, I knew very little about homeless men, or their problems, or how to help them.

I discovered very quickly that, according to government statistics, between thirty and thirty-five percent of homeless men suffer with Schizophrenia, and another thirty to thirty-five percent struggle with other mental illnesses. That means that about two out of every three homeless men struggle with some form of mental illness.

And because these men were homeless, they were not taking their medication, and so they were displaying aggressive behavior, paranoia, hearing voices, and other side effects of both mental illness and demonic activity. Also, because they were not eating properly, they were suffering from many different types of health issues.

So, I asked God for a plan, and He gave us one.

First, we developed a daily routine for the men, since we discovered that people with mental illness need consistency.

Then, at six am every morning, the night shift-worker prayer-walked around the mission, praying for physical and mental healing, binding all demonic spirits, and releasing the peace of God.

We got the men up every morning at seven am, taught them proper hygiene, got them showered, and gave them a warm cup of coffee. At eight am we fed them breakfast, and as they stood in line, we read healing scriptures over them, and prayed God's peace on them.

At ten am every morning, the day staff had a prayer meeting, and prayed for the men by name. At lunch time, we again read healing scriptures over them, and prayed God's peace over them.

At two pm, the day shift-worker prayer walked around the mission, praying for physical and mental healing, binding all demonic spirits, and releasing the peace of God.

At supper time, we again read healing scriptures over them, and prayed God's peace over them.

At ten pm, the men went to bed, and the evening shift-worker prayer-walked around the mission, praying for physical mental healing, binding all demonic spirits, and releasing the peace of God.

And oh yes, we also cast out demons whenever we discovered one.

Within a month of every new man coming to the mission, their behavior started to stabilize, and they began functioning in a balanced manner. Within three months of every new man coming to the mission, we were able to begin to lower their medication to a more acceptable level (with their doctor's permission), so that they could experience clarity of mind and emotions.

And within nine months of every new man coming to the mission, we were able to help them get at least a part-time, but often a full-time job (unless they were of retirement age). But even some of the retired men were able to secure part-time jobs.

Within that first year, we were told we were the most effective organization dealing with men with mental health illness, and we were asked to become part of the regional Mental Health Association task force. Unfortunately, after a couples of months we were asked to leave, when they discovered that our success was due to prayer and Bible reading.

6. Physical Illness

A woman in our congregation had a young son, about six years old, whose body was producing too much iron. As a result, his body was giving him iron poisoning, and killing him. The doctors tried a number of drugs in order to suppress his iron production.

He had to be hooked up to a special bag of medications every night while he slept. After a few weeks, they had to hook him up every evening as well as every night. Eventually, after a few months, he had to wear a special backpack, to stay hooked up to the medications even while at school. Unfortunately, even with twenty-four-hour medication, his body stopped responding to the treatments, and the doctors said that he would be dead within a matter of months.

We taught his mother how to lay hands on him before school every morning, and declare healing scriptures over him, and pray God's peace on him. Then, during the day, she would prayer-walk around the home, praying God's peace and healing over the home, and especially in his bedroom.

When her son got home after school, she would again pray healing scriptures and God's peace over him, and when he went to bed, she would pray healing scriptures and God's peace over him and prayer-walk around the home.

To the doctor's surprise (and even to us), within only a matter of days, his condition began to turn around. The doctors were in shock – they called it a miracle because they had stopped all treatments, and yet he was now improving. As of the writing of this eBook, this young man is in his mid-twenties, and is still doing well.

7. Building "Cleansing"

One of the things we do as a congregation is called "spiritual house cleansing". A team of two or three people (or more, if it is a serious situation) goes into a house or business, to spiritually cleanse it of all unhealthy spiritual activity.

First, we prayer-walk through the building, asking God to show us anything that needs to be repented of, or prayed for, taking notes in each room as we prayer-walked. Then, we gather together as a team, and share our notes and prayer insights.

Then, we pray a personal cleansing prayer, and have the head of the household or business pray a prayer of repentance for all unrighteousness done in the building, if needed.

Then we go from room to room, repenting from what God has shown us, praying for what God has shown us, commanding all demonic spirits to leave, and dedicating that room to the Lord.

At the end, we pray a final prayer of dedication for the building.

Over the years, because of this building cleansing, we have seen sin exposed, peace come upon homes, marriages restored, children brought back to Christ, strife resolved in homes and businesses, contentious employees removed, and blessing come upon homes and businesses.

Conclusion

God has given us a powerful tool, called "prayer-walking", and we can use it to:

* Change the spiritual atmosphere in our home, neighbourhood and workplace.

* Exercise our spiritual authority over the realm that God has called us to.

* Pull down spiritual strongholds.

* Set our loved ones spiritually, emotional, and physically free.

But to be effective, we must do four things as we prayer-walk:

1. Identificational Repentance

We must repent of personal sin, and on behalf of any evil done in that place.

2. Inspired Revelation

We must seek God's prayer insights for that place.

3. Spiritual Warfare

We must use our spiritual authority to pull down strongholds in that place.

4. Territorial Possession

We must dedicate that place for the Kingdom of God, and displace any demonic spirits, by commanding them to leave.

May God bless you, speak to you, and give you much revelation, as you begin to transform your territory, through Prayer-Walking.

Prayer-Walking Strategy - Summary

1. Identificational Repentance

   a) Cleanse our own hearts of all unrepented sin.
   b) Repent on behalf of all known unrighteousness being allowed in the area.
   c) Ask God to give us insight into other things that need repentance.

2. Inspired Revelation

   a) Continually ask God for insight on our area as we prayer-walk and pray for what He shows us.

3. Spiritual Warfare

   a) Walk in right relationship and unity with our prayer-walking partner.
   b) Declare that strongholds must come down, in Jesus' name.
   c) Thank God for the victory that He is working in the place we are prayer-walking.

4. Territorial Possession

   a) Claim and dedicate every place where we are prayer-walking, for the Kingdom of God.
   b) Command all unwanted spirits and evil doers to be displaced from the area.

Appendices

How To Begin Your Journey With God

John 14:6, NIV - *Jesus answered, "I am the way and the truth and the life. No one comes to the Father except through me.*

Living a life in partnership with God, through His Son Jesus, is the greatest adventure any person can ever experience. How can we make the initial decision to trust Him with our whole life, and begin to live for Him? It is as easy as A-B-C-D!

A – Admit that Jesus is indeed the only way to salvation, and that our hearts are completely lost without Him. (Romans 3:23, Romans 3:10).

B – Believe that Jesus died on the cross for our sins and rose from the dead for our freedom. (John 1:29, John 3:16-18, Acts 4:12).

C – Confess Jesus as our personal Lord and Saviour, the new leader of our lives. (Romans 10:9, John 5:24, John 1:12-13).

D – Decide to follow Jesus daily, and do what He asks of us. (Luke 9:23-24).

PRAYER

We can make those four choices, by saying a prayer something like this:

Jesus, I realize that I am lost without You, and You are the only way that I can experience freedom.

Thank You for dying on the cross to save me from the penalty of sin, and for rising from the dead so that I could be completely free.

I choose to confess and put my trust in You as my Lord and Savior. I give my whole heart and my whole life to You.

I ask You to indwell me by Your Holy Spirit, so that I can have Your help to do my best to follow You and please You each and every day.

In Jesus' name I pray. Amen!

Who Is David R. Hibbert?

David R. Hibbert grew up on the edge of a farm in rural Ontario, just north of London. After graduating from the University of Western Ontario, he worked as an Electrical-Mechanical Maintenance and Design Engineer in Hamilton, Ontario, before accepting the call to full-time Christian ministry.

During Bible school training in Peterborough, Ontario, he spent his summers as an interim Pastor in Northern Ontario. Upon graduation, he served as the Director of a Men's Mission for two years.

Then, at the leading of the Holy Spirit, he moved to the South Shore of Montreal, Quebec, Canada to plant a church and develop an Apostolic Centre.

He enjoys teaching, exhortation, short-term missions and developing training courses, books, and manuals. His Mission Statement is "to build, equip, and release purpose in people's lives."

He is married to an incredible woman named Kathleen, and has four grown awesome children – Kristen, Thomas, Kaylea and Elissa – as well as a growing number of grandchildren.

Other Books And Courses By David R. Hibbert

Note: These books are available around the world as paperbacks through Amazon, and as eBooks through Amazon and www.DestinyResource.ca.

Answering The BIG Questions

Every few years it is good to check our foundations, to see if there are any cracks in them, or if they have shifted because of the pressures of life.

"Answering The BIG Questions" is a new and fresh look at the really BIG questions of life, to ensure that our lives are still built on a good foundation. We look at God's Original Purpose, Understanding What We Lost, Understanding What We Really Need, Understanding How The Spirit Conforms Us, Understanding Our New Identity, and Understanding How To Live in Victory. A refreshing and liberating study of how to live as a child of God.

Building An Apostolic Centre

In this book we will develop an understanding of what an Apostolic Centre is, how the early church grew because of Apostolic Centres, and what are the basic ingredients that are necessary to ensure the establishment of a healthy Apostolic Centre that will bless the region and advance the Kingdom of God within that region.

Christmas Quizzicles

This eBook is a collection of some quizzes, games, stories, and inspirational notes – some serious, some thought-provoking, and some just plain silly. They are just a sampling of the many that I have collected over the years ... fun resources for children of all ages. May you enjoy them as much I have enjoyed collecting them.

These quizzes are great for family gatherings, small groups, church parties and more. Simply copy, hand out, and let the fun begin. Now have fun and celebrate!

Developing An Intentional Culture For Your Church, Business Or Family – Determining Your Relational Atmosphere

A culture is the relational atmosphere that every organization must have, in order to be healthy and effective. In this book David Hibbert explains the critical importance of planning, documenting, and promoting the desired culture. Although this book is written primarily for church communities, it applies equally as well to any group where people must work and co-exist together.

Discovering Your P.U.R.P.O.S.E.: Volume I – Developing A Personal Mission Statement

You have a purpose, a destiny, a special assignment from God Himself! And when you discover that purpose, commit to that purpose, and make decisions in alignment with that purpose, the Creator of the universe ensures that all of the resources in heaven and earth are directed toward you, so that you can fulfill that purpose.

There are seven primary indicators that God has given you, to help you discover what is your purpose in life. In Volume One of "Discovering Your P.U.R.P.O.S.E.", you will be taught the first two indicators to discover what is your purpose, and then be guided, step by step, to developing your own personal Mission Statement for your life, that you can use to help you stay on track, and make the best decisions for your life's purpose.

This Book can change the direction and focus of your life!

Discovering Your P.U.R.P.O.S.E.: Volume II – Realizing Your Specific Assignment

You have a purpose, a destiny, a special assignment from God Himself! And when you discover that purpose, commit to that purpose, and make decisions in alignment with that purpose, the Creator of the universe ensures that all of the resources in heaven and earth are directed toward you, so that you can fulfill that purpose.

There are seven primary indicators that God has given you, to help you discover what is your purpose in life. In Volume Two of

"Discovering Your P.U.R.P.O.S.E.", you will discover your Reoccurring Experiences, Personality Traits, Overriding Motivations, Spiritual Gifts and Extra Resources that you have, that will help you to fine-tune your purpose into a specific area of God-given assignment.

This Book can change the direction and focus of your life!

Embracing The Fivefold Ministry – Volume I – Introduction To The Fivefold Ministry

In this introduction to the fivefold ministry, you will discover the purpose of the fivefold ministries, their differences, how they work together in a church service, what happens when a church is only one-fold or two-fold, and church government in a fivefold church.

Embracing The Fivefold Ministry – Volume II – Understanding The Apostolic Ministry

Coming soon!

Embracing The Fivefold Ministry – Volume III – Understanding The Prophetic Ministry

Coming soon!

Experience Resurrection Power: By Embracing The Cross

In this Book, David Hibbert looks at the three parts of the cross; the vertical board, the horizontal board, and the foot of the cross, to explain the three most important things that Jesus did on the cross for us. He also shares a little understood consequence of Jesus' work on the cross that is indispensable to embrace, if we are going to truly experience Christian maturity in our lives. He clearly describes what must happen when we come to the cross if we want resurrection power in our lives. He also shares an amazing fact about an overlooked Christian ordinance that was designed by God to give us a special impartation of grace for experiencing resurrection power.

Fasting Made (Super) Simple

Biblical fasting has been very much misunderstood by many, if not most people. Because of that, for those who have tried to fast, and seen minimal or no results, it has left a poor impression on them. In this eBook you will be given very simple step-by-step and practical information on how anyone can fast, as well as the hidden key to fasting that will unlock its power for your life. Get ready for breakthrough!

F.E.A.R.L.E.S.S. – Eight Keys To Overcoming Fear

Fear is one of humankind's greatest enemies. At the least, it hinders and limits us. At the most, it keeps us in bondage, and plays havoc on our health, our relationships, and our potential. In this book David Hibbert gives you 8 keys to help you overcome every fear in your life.

Feasting On Christ's Grace At His Table

God has lovingly provided for His children, many sources of His amazing grace. Come and understand, and receive, the incredible grace of God that is available to each one of us, when we recognize it, and learn how to receive it, through the celebration of the Lord's Supper, also known as the Lord's Table, or Communion.

Five Keys For Effective Prayer Evangelism

In this book, David Hibbert shares with the reader five rarely used keys for praying for those who do not yet know Christ, or who have wandered away from faith in Christ. The task of bringing people to Christ is not just about preaching the gospel, it is also about waging spiritual warfare against Satan's tactics that affect a person's mind and heart and spiritual sight. Apply these five Biblical keys and see your prayer effectiveness reach a whole new level!

Forgiveness – The Key To Freedom

Forgiveness is such a really big deal! So many people struggle with unforgiveness, resentment, and personal wounds caused by others. And it is keeping so many people sick, limited, bound up, and side-tracked. God wants us to be free. Jesus died so that we can be free. But until we learn how to forgive, and live a life of forgiveness towards others, we will never be free.

This book looks at the topic of forgiveness ... what it is, what is isn't, why is it difficult to forgive, why we need to forgive, Biblical mindsets that help us forgive, and how we can truly forgive, so that we can be completely free in our lives.

Healing Father Wounds

Most Christians today have so much knowledge about Jesus, and yet we tend to be ineffective and unproductive. Why is this so? Because we are lacking certain qualities in our lives, because of father wounds. So, we need to have our father wounds healed, so that our knowledge can be translated into effectiveness.

In this book, you will discover what father wounds are, how you received your father wounds, how they affect your life, and God's amazing plan to re-parent you, so that you can be healed from all of your father wounds, and become the effective son or daughter of God that you were created to be.

Healing It's Yours

In this book David Hibbert uses much Biblical support to tackle the question, "It is always God's will to heal?" He then challenges us to consider that we may the solution to our own healing. Next, he presents many practical scriptures and examples to understand both keys to healing, and how to keep your healing. A very practical and Biblical explanation of healing for today.

How To Experience True Freedom

God wants us to become truly free. He wants us to experience the fullness of His forgiveness today, and He wants us to be free so that we do not repeat the cycle of failure in our lives.

This book will give you the understanding and tools you need to experience true freedom in your life. Experience true freedom from all guilt and shame and remorse, as well as damaged emotions from the offenses of others.

How To Gather Purposefully

When Christians meet together on a Sunday, why are they meeting? What is their goal? What do they expect to accomplish? Does God have any expectations from them?

This message will help Christians to understand how to meet with purpose and intention, so that God is truly glorified, His will is accomplished, and people are blessed by God as they meet. This message is very encouraging, practical, and brings much clarity to the gather of the local church.

How To Have A Healing Ministry

God wants every believer in Christ to share the love of Christ, minister to those who are suffering, and invite people into the Kingdom of God. The ministry of healing is a powerful tool to open hearts to the gospel. In this teaching, David Hibbert details ten keys that are necessary for anyone wanting to have a sustainable healing ministry. He also shares a proven ten step checklist for connecting with the sick, receiving permission to pray for them, and maximizing healing results. Very insightful, practical, and challenging.

How To Hear God's Voice – Five Keys For Clarity

Every Christian wants to know God's will, but to know the fullness of God's will, we need to be able to hear His voice.

In this book, you will be given a simple, yet very effective strategy for hearing God's voice. You will be amazed at how easy it is for you to hear God's voice. And you will be motivated to begin a life-long journey in daily hearing His voice and live in a new level of effectiveness in your walk with God.

How To Intercede For Your City

If we are a Christian, each one of us has a divine mandate to bring the gospel to our city. But we are often unsure what to do, how to do it, and how to be effective in doing it.

In this book you will learn how to intercede for your city, in a way, that you will actually see some results. This book is very practical, and includes information on the Biblical definition of nations, recent data on unreached and unengaged people groups, and statistics on migration from rural to city.

How To Self-Publish An eBook In Canada

For all of the aspiring authors out there, here is a very clear and simple explanation of the steps necessary to self-publish an eBook in Canada. Included in this book is information on the types, categories and main formats of eBooks, guidance on how to write an eBook, obtaining an ISBN number, opening an Amazon Kindle Direct Publishing Account, preparing, and publishing your eBook, and more.

Keys To Intimacy – Experiencing The Heart Of God

There is no trust without intimacy. Intimacy builds trust. In this series you will learn eight simple keys that will enable you to deepen your relationship with the lover of your soul and come to trust Him in a whole new way.

Learning How To Love: Manifesting Agape

Most of us still experience conflicts and offenses and damaged relationships. If love truly is as powerful a force as we say it is, then we must be willing to ask a very serious question: "Do we really know how to love?" This book examines the different types of love, gives a thorough description of the highest form of love, and then presents simple strategies to develop the skills necessary to express this amazing love – God's love.

Making The Most Of The Christmas Season: Inspiration For A Great Christmas And An Awesome New Year

Christmas can be a CRAZY time. Planning for family gatherings, getting presents for those we love, reconnecting with friends, navigating through Christmas and Boxing Day (now boxing week) sales, and not to mention the dreaded "year-end" inventory lists and financial statements. What on earth happened to "Merry Christmas and a Happy New Year"?

In this book, the reader will be presented with five strategies to make Christmas both meaningful and enjoyable and be able to face the New Year with hope and expectation. In all, these five strategic attitudes are easily implemented, and can make the difference between year-end panic, and year end hope for an even better year ahead.

Natural Discipleship

We are first and foremost children of God, and we become children of God the moment we become a Christian, and we are immediately placed into the family of God. So, what if our growth to maturity is not agreement to a list of doctrinal statements, and a development of good Christian habits? What if our spiritual growth as Christians actually follows the same process as the natural growth of children into adulthood.

This book will show you how the best way to mature in Christ, is to follow the same five steps as natural growth of every child into adulthood.

No Fear – Choose Peace And Grow Stronger In A Time Of Crisis

In this book, published during the COVID-19 pandemic of 2020, David Hibbert presents a Christian perspective on crisis, and then shares a number of important principles on how to face a crisis as a Christian, including how to do spiritual warfare during a crisis, how to pursue and fulfill your God-given purpose during a crisis, how to grow spiritually during a time of crisis, and how to stay in the peace of God during a crisis. This book will give you very practical tools so that you can go through the storm and come out even stronger.

Overcoming Fear In A Time Of Crisis – 28 Truths To Exchange Fear For Peace

This book was birthed in the middle of the COVID-19 pandemic of 2020, but the truths in it can equally apply to any pandemic or crisis in our lives. God's Word is applicable to every situation, and so this book will help you whether you are facing another world-wide epidemic, or a more focused personal crisis.

Read each chapter, consider it, meditate on it, and be encouraged. God is with you in your storm, and He will bring you to the other side!

Overcoming Self-Deception

When I first became a Christian, it seemed like everyone I met was concerned about doctrinal error. Do we believe the right things about the doctrine of the Holy Spirit, do we believe the right things about salvation, do we believe the right things about Jesus, do we believe the right things about the end times? In those early days, most error seemed to revolve around our interpretation of the scriptures. Today, however, much of the error that I have come across is not due to our interpretation of the scriptures, but due to our philosophy of how we even approach the Scriptures.

In this short book, I will look at what I believe is one of the most widespread errors in the church today, and then present a principle that will bring balance back to this error, as well as serve as a tool to avoid other errors in the future.

Overcoming The Orphan Stronghold

We believe that every Christian wants to be "fully conformed to the image of Christ" – they want to become all that they were created to be, and to fulfill their destiny here on earth.

However, every person on earth, including Christians, struggles with the orphan stronghold. It affects our faith in God, our ability to trust God, our ability to trust people, our ability to relate with others, our ability to have healthy marriages, our freedom in Christ, our healing, and even our destiny.

In these lessons, you will learn what the Orphan Stronghold is, where it came from, how it operates, how it manifests in us, and how we can begin to overcome it. God wants us free to be fully alive in Him!

Receiving The Seven-Fold Spirit Of God

In this book you will discover why most people, including many in the Pentecostal and Charismatic theological streams, have missed the full benefits of Pentecost. You will also discover what is the Seven-Fold Spirit of God, and how to embrace the fullness of the Holy Spirit. Get ready for breakthrough!

Seven Keys To Maturity In Christ

Most Christians want to grow in Christ, and to become mature Christians. But how is that accomplished? In this book we present seven keys that you can use to jump-start, and even quicken your Christian growth, as well as guarantee continued growth for the rest of your life. Learn how to apply the Keys of Liberty, Conformity, Identity, Authority, Clarity, Community, and Intimacy and discover the joy of maturity in Christ.

The Blessing Of Personal Prophecy

In this book, David Hibbert defines prophecy, public prophecy, and personal prophecy, and then validates Biblically that God uses people to minister personal prophecy today. Finally, he gives very practical guidelines for receiving, understanding, and responding to a personal prophetic word.

This book will answer the questions: What is Prophecy? Is Prophecy Still Valid Today? What Is The Purpose Of Prophecy? Our Response To Prophecy. How To Maximize The Blessing Of Your Prophecy. What Should Be Our Response To Prophecy? How To Maximize The Blessing Of Your Prophecy.

The Four Pillars Of Christian Maturity

In this book, David Hibbert looks at the Four Pillars Of Christian Maturity, as outlined in Acts 2:42-47. He explains each of the four pillars, and then gives practical examples of why they are so important to our spiritual health and maturity. He also gives a graphic example of what will happen to our spiritual life if we neglect these four pillars.

The Power of a Blessing

Every human being longs for love, longs for acceptance, longs for the knowledge that they are valued by someone, and that they have a purpose worth living for. God has given us the principle of blessing as a way to deposit within a person's heart, the assurance of all of these things. Learn how to transform a person's life for greatness, with your words and actions, in this simple five-part Biblical principle.

The Search For A Father: The Story Of David

In this insightful book, you will experience an intimate examination of David's search for a father, from his infancy, as a teen, and into his adult years. You will discover the cause of much of his failure, the source of much of his pain, and the secret of his later years of success. And you will conclude that he found what we all need, the presence of a godly father.

When Christians Face Crises

Why did this happen? Why did God allow it? Does God really care? These are some of the many questions that are asked "When Christians Face Crises". This book is not about religious platitudes are simplistic arguments. Instead, the writer seeks to give clear, Biblical answers to our very difficult questions concerning pain and suffering. This book will give the reader a compassionate and Biblical perspective on suffering and inspire hope to those presently in the midst of a crisis.

End Notes

1 https://theisraelbible.com/biblical-boundaries-land-israel/

Made in the USA
Columbia, SC
12 May 2024

35575736R00048